Behind the Mask: The Zodiac Killer

Behind the Mask: The Zodiac Killer

Behind The Mask

Will Anderson

Published by Oliver Lancaster, 2023.

While every precaution has been taken in the preparation of this book, the publisher assumes no responsibility for errors or omissions, or for damages resulting from the use of the information contained herein.

BEHIND THE MASK: THE ZODIAC KILLER

First edition. July 8, 2023.

Copyright © 2023 Will Anderson.

ISBN: 979-8223095682

Written by Will Anderson.

Also by Will Anderson

Behind The Mask
Behind the Mask: Amanda Knox
Behind the Mask: Jeffrey Dahmer
Behind the Mask: Ted Bundy
Behind the Mask: The Devil's Architect H. H. Holmes
Behind the Mask: The Golden State Killer
Behind the Mask: The Zodiac Killer
Beyond the Headlines: Unraveling the Menendez Brothers

Standalone
The Hatton Garden Heist: Unveiling the Greatest Jewel
Robbery in History

inclusion of brief quotations in a review.

By proceeding to read this book, the reader acknowledges and accepts the statements made in this disclaimer.

3

Chapter 1: Exploring the Emergence of the Zodiac Killer as One of America's Most Notorious Unsolved Mysteries

The late 1960s bore witness to a series of horrifying events that shook the very fabric of society in Northern California, birthing an enigma that would evolve into one of America's most notorious unsolved mysteries: the case of the Zodiac Killer.

The scene opens in the tranquil surroundings of the Bay Area, a region famous for its iconic landmarks, booming economy, and liberal values. It was here, amidst the undercurrent of social and political revolution, where the Zodiac Killer emerged as a malevolent shadow, sowing fear and casting a dark veil over the community.

The crimes began in December 1968. The scene of the first confirmed incident was a lovers' lane in Benicia, a small town located in the San Francisco Bay area. Here, two high school students, Betty Lou Jensen and David Faraday, were found shot dead. The mysterious execution, devoid of apparent motive, sent shockwaves through the otherwise peaceful community. Little did they know, this was just the beginning.

Seven months later, another couple, Darlene Ferrin and Michael Mageau, were attacked in Vallejo's Blue Rock Springs Park.

While Mageau managed to survive, Ferrin was not as fortunate. The attacker, an unknown man, slipped back into the shadows, leaving behind a gruesome tableau of horror and a mystery that was starting to unfold. Only a few hours later, the Vallejo Police Department received an anonymous call. The caller, claiming responsibility for both attacks, provided details that only the perpetrator could know. The Zodiac Killer had announced his arrival.

What distinguished the Zodiac Killer from other serial killers of the time was his audacious communication with the media. Weeks after the Vallejo incident, letters arrived at the offices of three Bay Area newspapers: The Vallejo Times-Herald, The San Francisco Chronicle, and The San Francisco Examiner. Each envelope contained one-third of a cryptogram and a chilling letter. The sender identified himself as 'Zodiac.' His communications bore a haunting symbol, a circle with a cross through it. The purpose of the cryptograms? A wicked game, it seemed, with the killer claiming they contained his identity.

The cryptic messages, the cold-blooded ruthlessness, the apparent lack of motive, and the grotesque pleasure he seemed to take in taunting the authorities with letters and coded messages all served to create a climate of palpable fear, which seemed to feed the Zodiac's need for power and control. The killings continued, with the perpetrator claiming up to 37 victims, although only five were confirmed.

As the years passed, the elusive spectre of the Zodiac Killer faded into the background, yet his legend grew in infamy. Despite the best efforts of law enforcement agencies and a myriad of amateur sleuths, the Zodiac Killer's true identity remains concealed behind the mask, a testament to the enduring enigma that continues to captivate the world's attention.

And so, we find ourselves delving into the depths of this grim mystery, immersing ourselves in the chilling narrative that unfolds. What drove the Zodiac Killer? How did he manage to evade capture? Is there a chance that the case could still be solved? All these questions and more will be explored as we journey into the shadows of one of America's most notorious unsolved mysteries.

The case of the Zodiac Killer has become a cultural phenomenon that extends far beyond the confines of true crime. It has infiltrated popular culture, psychology, and sociology, becoming a topic of public fascination and scholarly inquiry. It is a dark symbol of the unknown and the elusive, offering an eerie reminder of humanity's fascination with the macabre.

Ever since the first cryptic letters landed in newspaper offices, the public has been gripped by the case. The fascination is partly due to the Zodiac himself, a figure who became a master puppeteer, seizing control of the narrative. He fueled public interest with his ciphers and tantalising clues, making people feel like they were a part of this grim detective story.

Moreover, the Zodiac Killer operated in a time of rapid social change and upheaval. The late 1960s and early 1970s were characterised by protest movements, the counterculture, and growing distrust in institutions. Against this backdrop, the Zodiac became a terrifying embodiment of society's anxieties and fears. It's no wonder that this era of turbulence would give birth to one of the most enduring mysteries of the century.

The Zodiac's influence permeated popular culture, making its way into books, films, and television. Robert Graysmith's two books, "Zodiac" and "Zodiac Unmasked," perhaps the most famous publications on the subject, were both bestsellers, illustrating the public's insatiable appetite for the story. David Fincher's critically acclaimed 2007 film "Zodiac" further cemented the killer's place in the cultural pantheon, and countless documentaries and television series have sought to analyse or demystify the case.

The rise of the internet further amplified the cultural impact of the Zodiac Killer. The web spawned a new generation of amateur sleuths who discussed, debated, and dissected every element of the case. Online forums and social media groups became hotbeds of speculation and theory crafting, fueled by a collective desire to solve the seemingly unsolvable mystery.

Yet, the cultural impact of the Zodiac Killer is not limited to entertainment and amateur investigations. In academia, the case has prompted discussions on criminal psychology, forensic science, and the media's role in publicising criminal activity. Scholars have examined the Zodiac's behaviour to understand the mind of a serial killer, and linguists and cryptographers have poured over his ciphers.

In the realm of law enforcement and forensic science, the Zodiac case continues to be a subject of study. It underscores the importance of evolving investigative techniques, highlighting both the successes and failures in the hunt for the Zodiac.

The public fascination surrounding the Zodiac case is a testament to our collective curiosity about the darker aspects of the human psyche. It forces us to confront our fears and anxieties, reminding us of the line that separates society from chaos. It is an unsolved puzzle, a morbidly alluring labyrinth that invites us to uncover its secrets, only to confront us with more questions.

In exploring the cultural impact and public fascination surrounding the Zodiac Killer, we don't just delve into the specifics of a chilling crime spree; we venture into a reflection on society, our fears, and our incessant pursuit of the truth, no matter how elusive it may be.

Chapter 2: The Birth of Evil: A Portrait of the Zodiac

The identity of the Zodiac Killer remains unknown. Consequently, we don't have verifiable information about his early life or background. Any attempt to profile his formative years would therefore be speculative, based on behavioural analysis, profiles developed by criminologists, and characteristics typically found in similar criminal cases.

Given these limitations, let's explore some common features in the backgrounds of known serial killers that might potentially apply to the Zodiac Killer. However, it's important to remember that these are conjectures, not established facts.

Based on studies of other serial killers, there's a high likelihood that the Zodiac experienced a troubled childhood, marked by abuse or neglect. Many serial killers exhibit a pattern known as the 'MacDonald triad' during their early years: bedwetting beyond a normal age, a fascination with fire setting, and cruelty to animals. These behaviours are sometimes seen as indicators of violent tendencies later in life, although this theory remains a point of contention among criminologists.

The Zodiac may have also faced struggles with a sense of identity and self-worth, possibly as a result of early life traumas, or feelings of abandonment or isolation. The adoption of the 'Zodiac' persona might be interpreted as a means of asserting control or creating an alter ego that possessed the power and significance he felt he lacked in his personal life.

Moreover, it's plausible that the Zodiac Killer was highly intelligent and exhibited above-average cognitive abilities from an early age. His cryptograms and ciphers, coupled with his ability to elude law enforcement, suggest a calculated, cerebral individual. Perhaps he showed a keen interest in puzzles or codes during his formative years. It's also conceivable that he displayed a morbid curiosity about death or violent crime, a trait that some other serial killers have exhibited during their early lives.

Despite these theories, it's crucial to bear in mind that predicting the emergence of a serial killer based solely on early life factors is far from an exact science. Multiple factors, including genetic predisposition, environmental influences, and personal experiences, intersect in complex ways to shape an individual's development.

Attempting to piece together the formative years of the Zodiac Killer is akin to navigating through a thick fog; we can make out vague shapes and possible trajectories, but the path remains elusive. The nature of his crimes suggests a deeply troubled individual whose past likely bore the scars of significant traumas or hardships. Yet, until the identity of the Zodiac Killer is definitively unveiled, these theories remain speculative and unconfirmed.

Delving into the mindset of the Zodiac Killer is a venture into the shadowy realms of criminal psychology. As we attempt to illuminate this darkness, we must acknowledge that our analysis is based on observation of the Zodiac's actions and communications, rather than any known personal or biographical information. We are, in essence, creating a psychological portrait from a series of disturbing brush strokes.

One of the most striking aspects of the Zodiac Killer's profile is his apparent need for attention and control. This characteristic is evident in his correspondence with the media, his cryptic ciphers, and his chilling habit of providing details only the murderer could know. This suggests a narcissistic personality trait, where an inflated sense of self-importance and a deep need for attention and admiration overshadow empathy for others.

Moreover, the Zodiac's correspondence with the media and his creation of complex ciphers suggest a high degree of intelligence and cunning. Many experts have posited that the Zodiac's pleasure did not derive solely from the act of killing but also from the thrill of the subsequent cat-and-mouse game with the authorities. This psychological phenomenon, often referred to as 'duping delight,' may have provided the Zodiac with a sense of superiority and thrill.

Another significant aspect to consider is the Zodiac's apparent lack of remorse or guilt. The cold, calculated manner of his crimes, combined with his taunting communications, suggest psychopathy or antisocial personality disorder. Individuals with these conditions exhibit a chronic and pervasive disregard for the rights of others, lack of empathy, and often demonstrate manipulative behaviour.

The Zodiac's choice of victims — typically young couples in secluded areas — could indicate issues with intimacy and interpersonal relationships. Some criminologists speculate that the act of killing may have served as a distorted form of establishing control over such relationships, perhaps compensating for perceived inadequacies or failures in his personal life.

The Zodiac also demonstrated a form of theatricality or dramatisation in his crimes, most notably in the Lake Berryessa attack, where he wore a hooded costume adorned with his signature cross-circle symbol. This costume, which served no practical purpose in the commission of the crime, suggests a desire for creating a certain image or persona and further underscores the Zodiac's need for attention and control.

Finally, the cessation of the Zodiac's known activities raises questions about what might have triggered such a decision. Did he feel that the risks of capture were growing too great? Did some life event or change in circumstances disrupt his murderous activities? Or perhaps, as some theories suggest, he may have been institutionalised or died.

Exploring the Zodiac Killer's psychological profile is a chilling journey into the mind of a deeply disturbed individual. While we can draw conclusions and theories from his known actions and communications, the full complexity of his motivations and mindset remains a mystery, much like the Zodiac himself.

Chapter 3: Letters from the Abyss: Cryptic Messages Revealed

The letters from the Zodiac Killer form a disturbing yet fascinating element of the entire Zodiac saga. These communiqués provide chilling insight into the killer's mind, offering a mix of cryptic puzzles, chilling taunts, and grim details of his crimes. To understand the Zodiac, we must delve into the themes and messages found within his ominous correspondence.

Assertion of Superiority and Control

THROUGHOUT HIS LETTERS, the Zodiac demonstrated an apparent need to exert control and establish superiority over law enforcement and the media. His letters frequently included crime scene details that only the killer could know, thereby proving his identity and reinforcing his control over the narrative. Additionally, the Zodiac's ciphers were a distinct method of demonstrating intellectual superiority, as he seemed to take pleasure in presenting puzzles that he believed could not be solved.

Desire for Recognition and Infamy

THE ZODIAC'S LETTERS illustrate a clear desire for recognition. He created his own persona, complete with a symbol and a name, which he used consistently. This deliberate branding suggests an individual craving notoriety and infamy. The Zodiac also seemed to revel in the public panic and media attention his letters generated, further fueling his urge for recognition.

Lack of Remorse and Empathy

THE ZODIAC'S LETTERS display a startling lack of remorse or empathy for his victims. His cold, matter-of-fact descriptions of the murders suggest a complete emotional disconnect from the horrific nature of his actions. This chilling lack of empathy is a common trait among psychopaths and sociopaths.

Threats and Intimidation

MANY OF THE ZODIAC'S letters contain threats aimed at the community or law enforcement. For instance, in a letter to The San Francisco Chronicle dated November 9, 1969, the Zodiac claimed that he would kill more people if the newspaper did not publish his cipher. This continual intimidation served to heighten public fear and augment the Zodiac's perceived power.

Cryptic and Symbolic Messaging

THE ZODIAC FREQUENTLY included cryptograms or ciphers in his letters, encrypted messages that he claimed contained his identity or additional details about his crimes. Although some of these have been decoded, others remain unsolved. The inclusion of these ciphers underscores the Zodiac's desire to toy with authorities and demonstrate his intelligence.

Analysing the Zodiac's letters provides an opportunity to peer into the mind of this enigmatic figure. While they offer some insights into his motives and personality, they also deepen the mystery, leaving us with an incomplete and enigmatic portrait of a killer who, despite his craving for infamy, remained hidden in the shadows.

Code Breaking Efforts: Exploring the Methods Used by Investigators and Codebreakers to Decipher the Zodiac's Cryptic Messages

ONE OF THE MOST ENIGMATIC aspects of the Zodiac Killer's persona was his use of cryptograms and ciphers, presenting complex puzzles to authorities and the public. The Zodiac's cryptic messages fueled the terror and mystique surrounding him, turning code breaking into a vital part of the investigation.

The Zodiac sent four primary ciphers, known as Z408, Z340, Z13, and Z32, named for the number of characters each contains. The challenge these ciphers posed to investigators and codebreakers was immense, resulting from their apparent complexity, potential misspellings or errors, and the possibility that the Zodiac might have used a unique, self-developed method of encryption.

The first cipher, Z408, was the only one definitively solved in the decades following the Zodiac's reign of terror. Just a week after it was sent, the cipher was cracked by a schoolteacher and his wife, Donald and Bettye Harden. The Hardens recognized that the killer likely used symbols to represent the most common letters in the English language — a technique known as frequency analysis. The Hardens' breakthrough led to the deciphering of a disturbing message in which the Zodiac claimed to be collecting "slaves" for the afterlife.

The remaining three ciphers, however, proved far more resistant to decryption efforts. The 340-character cipher, known as Z340, stood as one of the most perplexing unsolved ciphers in criminal history until its reported decoding in December 2020. This breakthrough was achieved by an international team of codebreakers using a combination of manual analysis and machine learning. They discovered that the message was written in a diagonal pattern and adjusted the columns to match this pattern, which finally unlocked the hidden message. However, the decoded message didn't reveal the Zodiac's identity, as was hoped, but it did reinforce the killer's lack of remorse and his dark perspective on his murderous actions.

The final two ciphers, Z13 and Z32, are particularly challenging due to their brevity. With so few characters, there are fewer patterns to analyse and more possibilities for each symbol, making it harder for codebreakers to confidently solve them.

The attempts to break the Zodiac's codes have not only involved traditional code breaking methods but also cutting-edge technologies. Cryptographers have used statistical techniques, pattern recognition software, and artificial intelligence algorithms in their efforts to crack the Zodiac's ciphers, demonstrating the evolving intersection of criminal investigation and technology.

The Zodiac's ciphers represent a unique aspect of the case that amplifies its mystique and enduring fascination. They embody the Zodiac's need for control and his desire to taunt the authorities, serving as grim puzzles in this dark chapter of criminal history.

19

Chapter 4: Hunting Grounds: The Zodiac's Territorial Prowess

The locations chosen by the Zodiac Killer for his attacks provide another layer of complexity and intrigue to the investigation. While the connection between these sites and the Zodiac's identity or motivations remains speculative, they do offer potential insights into his methods and psychology.

The Zodiac's known attacks occurred in or near the San Francisco Bay Area, predominantly in secluded or romantic spots, often frequented by young couples. These locations included Lake Herman Road in Benicia, Blue Rock Springs Park in Vallejo, Lake Berryessa in Napa County, and Presidio Heights in San Francisco.

The choice of such settings could point to several aspects of the Zodiac's motivations or identity. The relative seclusion of these sites suggests a familiarity with the local area and a strategic choice to avoid detection. The perpetrator was able to approach and leave the scenes undetected, suggesting a level of premeditation and planning.

The Zodiac's focus on young couples suggests a particular fixation or trigger related to romantic relationships. It's speculated that this might indicate feelings of jealousy, rejection, or a need for power over such situations. Additionally, it's possible that couples provided a dual satisfaction for the Zodiac

— control over two victims simultaneously and heightened fear, as each victim witnessed the other's plight.

Of all the locations, the Lake Berryessa attack stands out due to the Zodiac's costume — a black hood and bib bearing his crossed-circle symbol. This theatrical element adds an additional layer of terror and indicates a desire to manifest his self-crafted persona physically. The relative remoteness of this site may have emboldened the Zodiac to take such a risk without being seen or identified.

Finally, the geographical clustering of his attacks might suggest that the Zodiac lived or worked in the San Francisco Bay Area, as most serial killers operate within a comfort zone close to their familiar locales. Some have theorised that his move towards urban San Francisco with the murder of cab driver Paul Stine might have indicated an increasing confidence or perhaps a change in his personal circumstances.

However, these analyses rely heavily on speculation and interpretation. Without conclusive evidence or a definitive identification of the Zodiac, the significance of the crime scene locations remains one of the many enigmatic aspects of the case.

23

Chapter 5: Investigators and Enigmas: Law Enforcement's Pursuit

The Zodiac Killer's modus operandi, the methods and patterns he employed in his crimes, provides a wealth of information for investigators. While there's no definitive conclusion that can provide a complete understanding of the Zodiac's motivations or identity, these patterns form an essential part of the puzzle.

Victim Selection

THE ZODIAC'S KNOWN victims were mainly young couples in isolated areas, with the exception of the murder of taxi driver Paul Stine. This pattern suggests a particular fixation or emotional trigger related to couples. It may also indicate the Zodiac felt more powerful or satisfied when generating fear in two victims simultaneously.

The deviation from this pattern in the Stine murder raises questions. Some believe it might represent a change in the Zodiac's personal circumstances, an escalation in his confidence, or a shift in his psychological state.

Location and Timing

THE ZODIAC'S ATTACKS were geographically clustered in the San Francisco Bay Area, suggesting that he operated within a comfort zone close to familiar locales. He chose isolated or semi-isolated locations, likely for privacy and to avoid detection.

The timing of the attacks also forms a noticeable pattern. Three of the four known attacks occurred late at night, providing additional cover and fewer potential witnesses. However, the Lake Berryessa attack took place in daylight, which again might indicate an escalation in the Zodiac's confidence.

Communication

THE ZODIAC'S COMMUNICATIONS were a significant part of his modus operandi. The taunting letters, the ciphers, and even the phone calls to police represent a need for attention, control, and a desire to instil fear. His signature symbol, the crossed circle, consistently appeared in his correspondence, emphasising the identity he had crafted.

Forensic Evidence

FORENSIC EVIDENCE COLLECTED from the crime scenes, including fingerprints, gun ballistics, and a handwriting analysis, also formed patterns but failed to conclusively identify the Zodiac. For instance, fingerprints collected at multiple scenes have yet to be definitively linked to any suspect.

Symbolism and Theatricality

THE ZODIAC EXHIBITED theatricality in his crimes, notably in his costume during the Lake Berryessa attack. This showmanship might reflect his narcissistic tendencies and his craving for infamy.

While the patterns and puzzles inherent in the Zodiac case offer tantalising clues, they also highlight the complexity and enigma that is the Zodiac Killer. Despite these insights, the killer's identity and motivations remain shrouded in mystery, underscoring the Zodiac case as one of the most baffling unsolved mysteries in criminal history.

The Zodiac case involved multiple law enforcement agencies and key personnel who contributed significantly to the investigation. Their varied approaches reflect the complexities of the case and the challenges posed by the Zodiac Killer.

Detective Dave Toschi, San Francisco Police Department

DETECTIVE DAVE TOSCHI was a central figure in the Zodiac investigation. Known for his flamboyant style and dedication, Toschi was the lead investigator in the murder of taxi driver Paul Stine, which became officially linked to the Zodiac case. Toschi's approach was dogged and detail-oriented; he was known to review case files tirelessly, seeking overlooked clues or connections.

Toschi favoured traditional detective work, pursuing leads, interviewing witnesses, and working closely with other jurisdictions. His approach was very much 'boots on the ground,' and he sought to develop a holistic understanding of the case.

Inspector Bill Armstrong, San Francisco Police Department

INSPECTOR BILL ARMSTRONG worked closely with Toschi on the Zodiac case. Armstrong was meticulous and calm, contrasting with Toschi's more flamboyant style. Armstrong's approach focused on managing the extensive case paperwork, cataloguing evidence, and coordinating with other departments.

Armstrong's methodical approach provided a crucial backbone to the investigation, ensuring that all information was accurately recorded and available for review. His focus on coordination was particularly vital in a case spanning multiple jurisdictions.

Detective Jack Mulanax, Vallejo Police Department

DETECTIVE JACK MULANAX led the investigation of the Zodiac's early attacks in Vallejo. Mulanax adopted an intensive, local approach, operating on the theory that the Zodiac was a Vallejo resident. He delved deep into the local community, interviewing potential witnesses and exploring local leads.

Mulanax's local focus led to several potential suspects, most notably Arthur Leigh Allen, who emerged as one of the most controversial figures in the Zodiac investigation.

Sheriff's Deputy Ken Narlow, Napa County Sheriff's Office

SHERIFF'S DEPUTY KEN Narlow led the investigation into the Lake Berryessa attack. Like Mulanax, Narlow focused heavily on the local angle, believing the Zodiac must have had a detailed knowledge of the area to select such a secluded spot for his attack.

Narlow's rigorous crime scene analysis yielded some key physical evidence, including a footprint and the Zodiac's bizarre 'costume,' which added a new dimension to the killer's profile.

Each of these investigators brought their unique skills and perspectives to the Zodiac case, contributing to the mosaic of information gathered about this elusive killer. Despite their efforts, the case remains open, underlining the enigma that is the Zodiac Killer and the monumental challenge he posed to law enforcement.

Difficulties Faced by Law Enforcement during the Zodiac Investigation

THE PURSUIT OF THE Zodiac Killer was an investigation fraught with challenges and roadblocks. From the lack of physical evidence to interagency cooperation to evolving technology, the detectives were in a continual struggle against a cunning adversary and the inherent complexities of the case.

Limited Physical Evidence

ONE OF THE MOST SIGNIFICANT challenges was the lack of conclusive physical evidence. Despite a few fingerprints attributed to the Zodiac, none could be definitively linked to any suspects due to the technology available at the time. The emergence of DNA technology later allowed investigators to attempt extracting DNA from the Zodiac's letters, but there has been no official confirmation of a DNA match to any suspects.

Interagency Cooperation

ANOTHER ROADBLOCK WAS the nature of the Zodiac's crimes, which spanned multiple jurisdictions. This required close cooperation between several police departments, each with its investigative styles and administrative policies. Sharing information and coordinating efforts across these different jurisdictions was a challenging process. The establishment of a centralised task force earlier in the case could have potentially improved information sharing and strategic coordination.

Lack of Clear Motive or Pattern

THE ZODIAC'S SEEMING lack of a clear motive or victim selection pattern also posed a significant challenge. While some patterns were identified, such as the focus on young couples, there was no obvious rationale behind his killings or his choice of victims. This unpredictability made it hard to anticipate his next move or develop a comprehensive profile.

Media and Public Involvement

THE EXTENSIVE MEDIA coverage and public fascination with the case presented another challenge. While it put pressure on law enforcement to solve the case, it also gave the Zodiac a platform from which to taunt investigators. Moreover, the high public profile of the case led to a deluge of tips and potential leads, many of which proved fruitless and consumed valuable investigative resources.

Technological Limitations

LASTLY, THE TECHNOLOGY available at the time of the Zodiac crimes was far less advanced than what law enforcement has at its disposal today. DNA profiling, advanced ballistics, digital databases, and surveillance technologies were either rudimentary or non-existent. The introduction of these resources could have potentially been game-changers in the hunt for the Zodiac.

While these challenges undoubtedly hindered the investigation, they also serve to underscore the complexity and enduring fascination of the Zodiac case. They demonstrate why, despite the tireless efforts of law enforcement and countless amateur sleuths, the Zodiac Killer's identity remains a mystery.

32

Chapter 6: The Cipher Breakers: Codebreakers and Armchair Detectives

The Zodiac Killer's cryptic messages sparked a unique response from the public that would see amateur codebreakers and armchair detectives take up the challenge of deciphering his codes. Their contributions have become a significant aspect of the Zodiac case narrative.

The Hardens

ONE OF THE MOST NOTABLE contributions came from Donald and Bettye Harden, a schoolteacher and his wife from Salinas, California. In August 1969, they cracked what is known as the "408 cipher," the Zodiac's first coded message sent in three parts to different newspapers. Their methodology involved looking for repeating symbols and guessing that the killer would be egotistical enough to start the message with 'I.' They then began recognizing patterns of symbols representing common English words, which ultimately led to the cipher's decryption.

The message, however, contained no useful information regarding the Zodiac's identity but rather a macabre statement about his supposed enjoyment of killing.

David Oranchak

FAST FORWARD TO 2020, another breakthrough was made by David Oranchak, a web designer and Zodiac cipher enthusiast. He, along with fellow amateur codebreakers Sam Blake, a mathematician in Melbourne, Australia, and Jarl Van Eycke, a Belgian warehouse operator and programmer, managed to decode the infamous "340 Cipher," which had remained unsolved for over 50 years.

They used a unique software program created by Van Eycke, which ran through 650,000 variations of possible ways the cipher could be read. After a painstaking process, they uncovered a readable message that began with the words "I hope you are having lots of fun in trying to catch me." The decoded message, like the earlier one solved by the Hardens, did not reveal any information that could help identify the Zodiac.

Other Contributions

BEYOND CODEBREAKING, many other amateur sleuths have contributed to the case by piecing together clues, researching potential suspects, and maintaining public interest in the Zodiac case. Some notable figures include Tom Voigt, who runs one of the most extensive Zodiac websites, and Robert Graysmith, whose books on the Zodiac case have kept the mystery alive in the public consciousness.

The efforts of these dedicated individuals underscore the public fascination with the Zodiac case. Their persistent efforts, spanning decades, reflect our collective desire to solve one of America's most enduring criminal mysteries.

Chapter 7: Suspects and Shadows: Unmasking the Zodiac

The emergence of the internet has dramatically transformed the landscape of crime-solving and investigation, fostering a global community of enthusiasts, experts, and curious minds dedicated to unravelling complex cases. The Zodiac case, with its cryptic letters and ciphers, proved to be a perfect match for this collaborative approach.

Crowdsourcing and Collaborative Problem-Solving

CROWDSOURCING INVOLVES leveraging the collective intelligence of a large group of people, often through the internet, to solve problems, generate ideas, or gather information. In the context of the Zodiac case, this approach has been used extensively, particularly in the realm of codebreaking.

Online platforms, forums, and websites dedicated to the Zodiac case have allowed enthusiasts worldwide to pool their resources, share theories, and cross-check information. This collective effort has resulted in breakthroughs that might not have been possible through individual efforts alone.

One notable example is the aforementioned decryption of the "340 Cipher." This was a global effort involving individuals from different countries, united by the internet, their interest in codebreaking, and the Zodiac mystery. Their successful collaboration demonstrated the power of collective problem-solving, especially when aided by modern technology.

The Role of Online Communities

BEYOND CODEBREAKING, online communities have played a crucial role in compiling and analysing information related to the Zodiac case. Websites like zodiackiller.com, managed by Tom Voigt, provide extensive archives of case files, suspect information, theories, and news. These platforms facilitate discussions among users, encouraging the exchange of ideas and theories.

Such collaborative efforts have kept the Zodiac case alive in public consciousness and continue to generate new leads and theories, even decades after the crimes were committed.

A New Paradigm in Problem-Solving

THE COLLECTIVE EFFORTS in tackling the Zodiac mystery highlight a new paradigm in problem-solving. As the digital world continues to connect people globally, the power of crowd-sourcing and collaborative investigation becomes ever more potent. It enables the pooling of diverse skills, perspectives, and knowledge, thereby increasing the chances of unearthing solutions to even the most complex mysteries.

In summary, while the Zodiac's identity remains elusive, the collective and persistent efforts of codebreakers and online communities worldwide exemplify a profound shift in how such mysteries can be approached, keeping the hope alive that one day this enigma might be unravelled.

Investigating the Individuals Who Have Been Considered as Potential Zodiac Suspects

OVER THE YEARS, SEVERAL individuals have come under scrutiny as potential Zodiac Killer suspects. The two most debated suspects have been Arthur Leigh Allen and Richard Gaikowski. While the case remains unsolved, the evidence and theories surrounding these men continue to fuel speculation and debate.

Arthur Leigh Allen

ARTHUR LEIGH ALLEN became a prime suspect following a tip-off from his friend, Don Cheney, who claimed Allen had expressed a desire to kill people and call himself "Zodiac" before the crimes were even committed. Allen, a former elementary school teacher, certainly cast an ominous figure. In addition to this tip-off, Allen was identified by surviving victim Michael Mageau in a photo lineup as the man who shot him and Darlene Ferrin.

Several circumstantial pieces of evidence linked Allen to the Zodiac. He owned the same caliber gun used in the Zodiac shootings, wore a Zodiac brand wristwatch, and was ambidextrous, which could explain the difference in handwriting styles seen in the Zodiac's letters. Allen also had a criminal record, including charges for child molestation, which showed his propensity for deviant behaviour.

However, despite this collection of circumstantial evidence, no physical evidence linked Allen to the Zodiac crimes. His fingerprints did not match those found at crime scenes, and despite several search warrants, no incriminating evidence was ever found at his residence. In 2002, a DNA comparison was made between a sample obtained from Allen after his death in 1992 and the partial genetic profile derived from the stamps and envelopes of the Zodiac letters. The results did not match, further casting doubt on Allen's guilt.

Richard Gaikowski

RICHARD GAIKOWSKI WAS a journalist and filmmaker who emerged as a potential Zodiac suspect primarily through the efforts of amateur sleuth "Blaine Blaine". Blaine claimed to have decoded Gaikowski's name from one of the Zodiac's ciphers and asserted that Gaikowski bore a striking resemblance to the composite sketch of the Zodiac. He also alleged that Gaikowski had a strange fascination with death and had access to information about the Zodiac killings through his work at a newspaper.

Yet, like Allen, the evidence against Gaikowski was largely circumstantial and speculative. There was no physical evidence linking him to the crimes, and his fingerprints did not match those found at the crime scenes. Similarly, DNA extracted from the Zodiac's letters did not match Gaikowski.

While the theories and evidence surrounding Allen and Gaikowski paint a compelling picture, the lack of conclusive evidence keeps them in the realm of speculation. It underscores the enduring mystery of the Zodiac case, where a plethora of suspects, theories, and pieces of evidence abound, yet a definitive answer remains elusive.

Unresolved Clues: Loose Ends in the Zodiac Case that May Lead to Future Breakthroughs

THE ZODIAC CASE IS awash with unresolved clues and unanswered questions that offer tantalising hints to the killer's identity. While no single lead has definitively unmasked the Zodiac, several loose ends merit continued attention and could potentially catalyse future breakthroughs.

Unsolved Ciphers

ONE OF THE MOST INTRIGUING aspects of the Zodiac case is the killer's use of coded messages. While several of these have been solved, the Z13 and Z32 ciphers remain uncracked. Both are significantly shorter than the solved ciphers and may not contain enough symbols for a reliable decryption. However, if a solution is ever found, it could offer a new piece of the Zodiac puzzle.

DNA Analysis

THE DEVELOPMENT OF advanced forensic techniques provides a promising avenue for future breakthroughs. The Zodiac Killer sent numerous letters to the media, and it's possible that some contain traces of his DNA. Despite several attempts, no conclusive DNA profile of the Zodiac has been established so far, but further advancements in DNA technology could potentially reveal a profile that could be matched to a suspect.

Unidentified Victims

THE ZODIAC KILLER CLAIMED to have killed as many as 37 people, but only five murders and two attempted murders have been definitively linked to him. Investigating these unsolved and potential Zodiac cases could reveal patterns or evidence that help identify the killer. An expansion of the victim list based on the killer's modus operandi and letter claims could potentially lead investigators to new crime scenes and evidence.

New Forensic Techniques

FORENSIC SCIENCE HAS come a long way since the time of the Zodiac murders. New techniques, such as geographic profiling and digital forensics, could offer new insights. Geographic profiling, for instance, could provide a better understanding of the killer's movements and potentially reveal his residence or place of work.

Digital Sleuthing

THE RISE OF THE INTERNET and the ensuing collaboration of online sleuths have already proven their worth in the Zodiac case, and this could be a significant source of future breakthroughs. The collective intelligence and problem-solving power of thousands of armchair detectives worldwide could lead to new theories, decoded messages, or even the identification of the killer.

BEHIND THE MASK: THE ZODIAC KILLER

While the Zodiac case remains one of America's most notorious unsolved mysteries, these unresolved clues and avenues of investigation keep alive the possibility of one day uncovering the true identity of the Zodiac Killer. The hunt for the Zodiac, it seems, is far from over.

42

Chapter 8: Survivors and Victims: The Lingering Trauma

Surviving a traumatic event like a Zodiac attack inevitably leaves a lasting mark. The survivors' stories not only provide critical insights into the Zodiac Killer's methods but also reveal the profound psychological impacts and the struggle to cope with the aftermath of their encounters.

Michael Mageau

MICHAEL MAGEAU WAS one of the two victims in the Blue Rock Springs shooting on July 4, 1969. While his companion, Darlene Ferrin, succumbed to her injuries, Mageau survived despite being shot multiple times. His identification of Arthur Leigh Allen in a photo lineup provided a significant lead in the case, even though it was years after the attack.

The trauma of the attack deeply impacted Mageau. He disappeared from public view for many years, perhaps in an attempt to escape the attention and reliving of the dreadful night. While little is known about how he coped with his trauma, his willingness to participate in the investigation decades after the event signifies an attempt to confront the past and contribute to the killer's capture.

Bryan Hartnell

BRYAN HARTNELL, ALONG with Cecelia Shepard, was attacked while picnicking at Lake Berryessa on September 27, 1969. Despite being stabbed multiple times, Hartnell survived, but unfortunately, Shepard did not. Hartnell's account of the Zodiac's bizarre costume and the conversation they had before the attack provided unique insights into the killer's mindset.

Hartnell displayed remarkable resilience in the face of his traumatic experience. He finished law school, embarked on a career in probate law, married, and started a family. He seldom spoke about his encounter with the Zodiac, a decision that seemed to serve him well in his recovery and move forward in life.

The Impact of Survival

SURVIVING SUCH A TRAUMATIC event often leads to Post-Traumatic Stress Disorder (PTSD), characterised by severe anxiety, flashbacks, and nightmares. Both Hartnell and Mageau would have had to grapple with the psychological effects of their encounters with the Zodiac.

Yet, in spite of their ordeals, these survivors symbolise resilience and the human spirit's capacity to heal and rebuild. Their stories serve as a potent reminder of the personal dimension of the Zodiac case, which extends beyond the tantalising puzzles and cryptic letters to real individuals whose lives were forever altered by a masked murderer whose identity remains shrouded in mystery.

The Zodiac Killer's crimes were not only acts of violence against individuals; they also wreaked havoc on families, friends, and communities that loved and cherished the victims. These losses, punctuated by the enduring mystery of the killer's identity, have fueled ongoing efforts to honour and remember the victims.

Remembering the Victims

MEMORIALS AND COMMEMORATIONS have served as important touchstones for families and communities to honour the victims. They provide a space to remember the individual lives lost, moving beyond the sensationalism of the Zodiac case and focusing on the personal narratives of those who were tragically taken.

One poignant example is the plaque at Lake Berryessa, near the site of Bryan Hartnell and Cecelia Shepard's attack. The plaque commemorates the incident and, importantly, Shepard's life. Similarly, David Faraday and Betty Lou Jensen, the first confirmed victims, are remembered through a memorial plaque at the site of their murders in Benicia, California. These sites of remembrance transform the locations from places of horror into spaces of collective memory and mourning.

Victims' Legacies

WHILE THE ZODIAC KILLER'S victims are remembered primarily in relation to the tragic circumstances of their deaths, their lives tell stories of their own. David Faraday, an Eagle Scout, was an enthusiastic participant in his school's marching band. Betty Lou Jensen was an honour roll student with a passion for music and the outdoors. Darlene Ferrin, a devoted mother, was known for her vibrant personality and love for painting. Cecelia Shepard was a graduate student in history, planning to devote her life to teaching others.

These snapshots of their lives underscore the profound losses inflicted by the Zodiac Killer. The victims were more than just names in an infamous case - they were individuals with dreams, passions, and people who cared about them.

Impact on Families

THE MURDERS COMMITTED by the Zodiac Killer have had long-lasting effects on the victims' families. Parents, siblings, children, and spouses have had to grapple with their loss under the harsh spotlight of public attention. Despite their grief, many have shown tremendous resilience and have been outspoken advocates for justice in the case. Their unwavering determination serves as a powerful testament to the love and memory of the victims.

While the Zodiac case is defined by its mystery, it is essential to remember the human cost at its core. The victims, remembered through memorials and their enduring legacies, are a poignant reminder of the lives cut short by a faceless killer. And in their memory, the pursuit for truth and justice continues.

Chapter 9: Pop Culture Phenomenon: The Zodiac in Media and Art

The enduring mystery of the Zodiac case, with its cryptic letters, uncracked codes, and unidentified killer, makes for compelling material in literature and true crime books. Authors have approached this enigma from various angles, each with its unique narrative style, focus, and interpretation. Such literary explorations have significantly influenced public perceptions and understanding of the case.

Robert Graysmith's "Zodiac" and "Zodiac Unmasked"

PERHAPS THE MOST WELL-known books on the Zodiac case are Robert Graysmith's "Zodiac" and its sequel "Zodiac Unmasked". Graysmith, a cartoonist for the San Francisco Chronicle when the Zodiac was active, spent years researching the case. His books, while providing an engrossing and detailed account, lean heavily toward Arthur Leigh Allen as the prime suspect. While some critique his methods and conclusions, there's no doubt that Graysmith's works have greatly influenced the popular narrative surrounding the Zodiac Killer.

Gareth Penn's "Times 17"

GARETH PENN'S "TIMES 17" presents a unique and controversial perspective on the Zodiac case. Penn, an amateur sleuth, introduces the concept of "radian theory", suggesting that the Zodiac murders were located on a radian on a map. His prime suspect, Michael O'Hare, however, has never been seriously considered by law enforcement. Despite its lack of acceptance in official circles, Penn's work underscores the case's complexity and its draw for amateur detectives.

Mark Hewitt's "Hunted: The Zodiac Murders"

MARK HEWITT'S "HUNTED: The Zodiac Murders" takes a different approach, focusing less on the identity of the killer and more on the actual crimes, the investigation, and the victims. His meticulous and factual account is a departure from the suspect-oriented narratives and provides a sobering perspective on the impact of the Zodiac's crimes.

Influence on Public Perception

EACH OF THESE WORKS, with their unique narratives and theories, shape the public's understanding and perception of the Zodiac case. Graysmith's conviction of Allen as the Zodiac might have introduced biases in some readers' minds. Conversely, Penn's radical theories and complex cryptographic work highlight the enigmatic nature of the case. Hewitt's focus on the victims rehumanizes the case, moving the attention from the killer to those who suffered at his hands.

Furthermore, these books' popularity has kept the Zodiac case alive in public memory. They feed into the fascination surrounding unsolved crimes and the desire to unmask the perpetrator. They show how the Zodiac Killer, through his cryptic correspondence and elusive identity, continues to grip the imagination, inciting fear, fascination, and a collective desire to solve the ultimate puzzle he left behind.

From Hollywood blockbusters to television docuseries, the Zodiac Killer's chilling saga has found a prominent place in the cinematic landscape. These adaptations offer varying interpretations of the case, with differing degrees of factual accuracy, narrative focus, and stylistic approach.

David Fincher's "Zodiac" (2007)

DAVID FINCHER'S "ZODIAC" is arguably the most notable and critically acclaimed cinematic exploration of the Zodiac case. It primarily follows the perspective of Robert Graysmith, a cartoonist who becomes obsessed with the case. The film is lauded for its meticulous attention to detail, accurately replicating crime scenes, and adhering to known facts of the case.

However, its fidelity to Graysmith's narrative and prime suspect - Arthur Leigh Allen - could be viewed as a limitation. While the movie does a commendable job depicting the frustration and obsession stirred by the Zodiac case, the exclusive focus on Allen somewhat oversimplifies the complexity of the investigation.

"The Zodiac Killer" (1971)

"THE ZODIAC KILLER," a low-budget film released while the real Zodiac was still active, stands as a historical artefact of sorts. The filmmakers' primary aim was to draw out the killer by hosting a premiere in San Francisco. As such, the film's strength lies less in its factual accuracy or production value and more in its audacious exploitation of ongoing events.

"The Zodiac" (2005)

"THE ZODIAC," DIRECTED by Alexander Bulkley, focuses on the impact of the Zodiac's reign of terror on the small community of Vallejo, California. While not as detailed or comprehensive as Fincher's "Zodiac," it offers a compelling look at the fear and paranoia that gripped the city.

However, this film's limitation lies in its characterization of the Zodiac. The portrayal leans heavily towards an anonymous, shadowy figure, creating a chilling but somewhat generic movie serial killer.

TV Docuseries: "The Hunt for the Zodiac Killer" (2017)

HISTORY CHANNEL'S "The Hunt for the Zodiac Killer" dives deep into the case with a blend of documentary and dramatic reenactment. It reinvigorates the investigation with new technology and code-breaking efforts. While the series provides an exciting and detailed account, it leans heavily into the speculative side, particularly with new and unverified theories.

Strengths and Limitations

CINEMATIC PORTRAYALS offer viewers an engaging and digestible format to understand the complex Zodiac case. However, they often simplify or dramatise events for narrative purposes, and can inadvertently bias viewers towards certain theories or suspects. Despite these limitations, they have played a significant role in maintaining public interest in the case and fostering a broader understanding of its implications.

Chapter 10: The Legacy Continues: The Zodiac's Unresolved Legacy

The Zodiac case, in its complexity and high-profile nature, has had a significant impact on criminal investigations, particularly in the realms of forensic science, criminal profiling, and the development of investigative protocols.

Forensic Science

THE ZODIAC CASE UNFOLDED during a transformative period in forensic science. Despite its challenges, it highlighted the importance of forensics in criminal investigations. For instance, one of the biggest forensic developments connected to the case is the analysis of handwriting and latent prints. Investigators used these techniques extensively in an attempt to identify the Zodiac, analysing letters he sent to various media outlets. Although they have yet to definitively identify the Zodiac, these techniques remain crucial in criminal investigations today.

Criminal Profiling

THE ZODIAC CASE SIGNIFICANTLY influenced the field of criminal profiling. In many ways, the Zodiac seemed to defy traditional patterns of criminal behaviour, killing victims in different locations, using varied methods, and deliberately engaging with law enforcement and media. The FBI and local police developed a psychological profile of the Zodiac, predicting his likely traits based on his behaviour. This helped to popularise criminal profiling, and many of the techniques used are still practised today.

Investigative Protocols

THE ZODIAC CASE DEMONSTRATED the need for better coordination between law enforcement agencies. The Zodiac struck in various jurisdictions, leading to difficulties in sharing information and resources effectively. This challenge sparked improvements in communication and collaboration between departments, emphasising the importance of unified databases and joint task forces in multi-jurisdictional cases.

Impact on Criminology and Criminal Justice Studies

THE ENIGMA OF THE ZODIAC Killer has also found its way into the academic realm, featuring in criminology and criminal justice studies. The case provides rich material for studying criminal behaviour, the effects of media interaction, and the public's reaction to high-profile unsolved crimes. It continues to intrigue and educate future law enforcement officers, investigators, and criminologists.

The Zodiac case, with its unique set of challenges and high-stakes puzzle, has been instrumental in refining investigative techniques and enhancing our understanding of criminal behaviour. Even though the case remains unsolved, its influence persists in the evolving landscape of crime-solving and criminal justice.

In recent years, the Zodiac case, despite its status as a "cold case," has seen renewed interest and progress, spurred by technological advancements, innovative investigative methods, and fresh perspectives.

Forensic Genealogy

ONE OF THE MOST EXCITING advancements in criminal investigations is forensic genealogy, a technique that helped identify the Golden State Killer in 2018. Using DNA from crime scenes and matching it with genetic information available in genealogical databases, investigators can identify potential relatives of an unknown suspect and work their way to the culprit. For the Zodiac case, this technique holds potential. If viable DNA can be extracted from any of the Zodiac's letters or other evidence, this method could bring us closer to uncovering the Zodiac's identity.

Digital Forensics and Cryptography

THE ZODIAC KILLER'S cryptic ciphers have long baffled both amateur and professional codebreakers. However, digital forensics and advanced cryptography software now offer new possibilities. For instance, in December 2020, a team of independent cryptographers finally cracked the Zodiac's 340-character cipher, known as the Z340, using advanced decryption software. While the decoded message didn't reveal the Zodiac's identity, it was a significant milestone and a testament to the potential of technology in decoding the remaining unsolved ciphers.

Crowdsourcing Investigations

ANOTHER CONTEMPORARY approach is crowdsourcing investigations, where information and hypotheses are shared and discussed among a large, online community of interested individuals. Websites and forums allow amateur sleuths to collaborate, share findings, and keep the case in the public eye. Though this can occasionally lead to misinformation and unfounded speculation, it also fosters an environment where fresh perspectives and ideas can emerge.

New Leads and Information

SOMETIMES, COLD CASES are revived due to new information or leads, often prompted by media coverage or renewed public interest. With the Zodiac case consistently in the public eye, it's possible that someone, somewhere, could provide a crucial piece of information that leads to a breakthrough.

While the Zodiac Killer case has frustrated investigators for decades, the advancements in investigative techniques, combined with a persistent public interest, keep the hope of solving this mystery alive. The final chapter of the Zodiac Killer's story may yet be written, and when it is, it will be the culmination of relentless investigative effort, technological innovation, and an unwavering belief in justice.

Chapter 11: The Unquenchable Shadows: Looking Forward

As we reflect on the journey into the heart of one of America's most infamous unsolved mysteries, we have ventured through the labyrinthine history of the Zodiac case, unearthing a myriad of insights and discoveries along the way.

The Cultural Impact

OUR EXPLORATION BEGAN with an examination of the cultural impact of the Zodiac case, highlighting how the unknown assailant's enigmatic persona and cryptic communications captured public imagination, sparking a fascination that has endured for more than half a century.

The Mystery Behind the Mask

THE EXPLORATION INTO the potential background and formative experiences of the Zodiac illuminated the possibilities of what could have influenced his later actions, even if the exact identity of the killer remains elusive. The various theories presented, ranging from a disrupted upbringing to potential military connections, provide intriguing lenses through which to view the Zodiac's disturbing actions.

Psychological Profiling

THE ANALYSIS OF THE Zodiac's psychological profile offered insights into the potential motivations driving his heinous crimes. His need for control, attention, and his disregard for human life painted a chilling picture of a profoundly disturbed individual.

Cryptic Communications

THE ZODIAC'S LETTERS and ciphers provided a window into his twisted mind. Themes of power, manipulation, and a perverse enjoyment in engaging with law enforcement were evident in his cryptic messages, reflecting a complex and frightening persona.

Innovative Investigative Methods

THE CASE CATALYSED significant advancements in investigative techniques, from forensic sciences to the use of criminal profiling and cross-jurisdictional collaborations. The Zodiac case remains a pioneering example of the potential of new technologies, from digital forensics to DNA profiling, in solving complex crimes.

Collaborative Efforts

THE ROLE OF AMATEUR sleuths and online communities was pivotal in maintaining interest in the case and contributing to its ongoing investigation. The collaborative decryption of the Z340 cipher stands testament to the power of collective intelligence in cracking even the most complex puzzles.

Unresolved Clues and Potential Breakthroughs

DESPITE SIGNIFICANT advances, intriguing unresolved aspects of the Zodiac case continue to tantalise investigators, from unbroken ciphers to unidentified DNA samples. These tantalising clues hold the promise of future revelations, maintaining the allure of this enduring mystery.

Throughout this book, we've delved into the chilling world of the Zodiac Killer, unmasking layers of complexity, intrigue, and horror. The journey, while often grim, has revealed profound insights into criminal behaviour, societal responses, investigative methodologies, and our collective fascination with unsolved mysteries. The case of the Zodiac Killer remains a haunting testament to the depths of human depravity and the relentless quest for truth and justice.

There's an inescapable allure that the Zodiac Killer holds over the collective consciousness, a captivation that's maintained its grip for over five decades. Despite the progression of time, the fascination with the Zodiac case persists, fueled by its intricate enigma, cultural resonance, and the ceaseless quest for resolution.

The Power of the Unresolved

HUMANS ARE DRIVEN BY a desire for understanding and closure. The Zodiac case, with its numerous unanswered questions, uncracked codes, and an unidentified perpetrator, defies this desire. The absence of resolution propels curiosity, prompting amateur sleuths and professional investigators alike to keep digging, to keep questioning. Every uncovered layer seems to add to the mystery rather than resolve it, creating a sense of an infinite puzzle.

A Symbol of Fear and Fascination

THE ZODIAC KILLER, through his cryptic letters and gruesome crimes, created a horrifying yet strangely mesmerising persona. This dread-inducing figure, who managed to elude capture while taunting the police and public, became a symbol of the ultimate boogeyman. This macabre fascination fuels countless books, movies, podcasts, and internet forums, further embedding the Zodiac into popular culture.

A Catalyst for Change

THE ZODIAC CASE SPARKED significant changes in investigative techniques and criminal justice practices. From advances in forensic science to the establishment of unified databases for information sharing among law enforcement agencies, the Zodiac's legacy extends into the realm of criminal investigation methods. This provides a level of professional and academic interest that goes beyond the sensational aspects of the case.

Crowdsourcing and Collaboration

THE EMERGENCE OF DIGITAL platforms and social media has enabled widespread collaboration and discussion around the case. The collective decoding of the Zodiac's ciphers and the sharing of theories and findings have given the case a new lease of life, attracting a younger audience and ensuring its continued relevance.

Hope for Closure

AT THE HEART OF THE continued interest in the Zodiac case is a hope for closure, both for the victims' families and the public. Each technological advancement, each new piece of information, reignites hope that the Zodiac's identity may finally be revealed, that justice may eventually be served.

The enduring fascination with the Zodiac Killer lies at the intersection of fear, curiosity, the human need for resolution, and the relentless pursuit of justice. The Zodiac case continues to captivate because it encapsulates a haunting narrative that defies understanding, a narrative that is as much a societal reflection as it is about a single, ruthless killer.

WILL ANDERSON

62

Chapter 12: Shadows in the Rearview: Lessons from the Zodiac

The ripple effects of the Zodiac Killer's reign of terror go far beyond his victims and their immediate circles, seeping into the fabric of society at large. His actions challenged law enforcement practices, reshaped public perceptions of safety, and inspired new strategies in crime prevention and investigation.

Public Consciousness and Perception of Safety

THE ZODIAC KILLER, with his calculated violence and terrifying communications, sowed fear and uncertainty in the hearts of Californians, and eventually, the entire nation. His actions sparked a fundamental shift in the public consciousness about personal safety and the nature of crime. Innocuous activities like parking in a lover's lane or hitchhiking became fraught with potential danger. The Zodiac symbolised the random, inexplicable violence that could strike anyone, anywhere, shattering the myth of safety in public spaces and leading to heightened public vigilance.

Law Enforcement Practices

THE ZODIAC CASE EXPOSED gaps and shortcomings in law enforcement procedures of the time. Jurisdictional issues, lack of effective communication between different police departments, and the absence of unified databases hampered the investigation. In response, law enforcement agencies started moving towards improved interdepartmental collaboration and data sharing. The creation of databases like CODIS for DNA evidence and the implementation of shared communication platforms are partly a legacy of lessons learned from the Zodiac case.

Moreover, the case underlined the importance of behavioural profiling in criminal investigations. The inability to definitively identify the Zodiac highlighted the need for a deeper understanding of criminal psychology, sparking interest in offender profiling, a practice that would later become a cornerstone in hunting serial killers.

Crime Prevention Strategies

THE ZODIAC'S CASE PROMPTED a reconsideration of crime prevention strategies. Public awareness campaigns were initiated to educate citizens about personal safety measures. These ranged from advising against stopping for strangers to promoting better awareness of one's surroundings. It was a turning point in public safety advocacy, heralding a shift towards proactive prevention strategies.

The Power of Media

THE ZODIAC CASE WAS a grim testament to the power of media in shaping public perception and amplifying fear. The killer's open communication with newspapers, his ciphers published and reported on widely, exemplified the media's role in crime narratives. While this brought attention to the case and incited public involvement, it also highlighted the ethical quandaries around granting criminals a public platform.

The Zodiac Killer's reign of terror had a profound societal impact, redefining perceptions of safety, transforming law enforcement practices, and prompting changes in crime prevention strategies. It's a chilling reminder that the actions of one individual can echo through society, prompting us to reevaluate our systems, confront our fears, and strive for a safer, more secure community.

Justice and closure are integral to healing for victims' families, survivors, and communities impacted by heinous crimes like those committed by the Zodiac Killer. The pursuit of justice in such cold cases presents a multitude of ethical considerations and challenges, manifesting in the realm of procedural hurdles, technological advancements, and the psychological toll on involved parties.

Balancing Justice and Rights

THE FIRST ETHICAL CONSIDERATION is the balancing act between seeking justice and respecting the rights of individuals under suspicion. In the quest for closure, it's crucial that investigations maintain respect for due process, privacy, and the presumption of innocence. As tempting as it might be to circumvent these principles for swift resolution, it's a cornerstone of our legal system that these rights are upheld even in the face of public pressure and societal demand for answers.

The Use of Advanced Technologies

THE ADVENT OF NEW INVESTIGATIVE technologies, particularly in the realm of DNA analysis and digital forensics, has offered fresh avenues for justice in cold cases. However, these techniques also pose ethical questions about privacy and consent. For instance, the use of genealogical databases to trace potential suspects—while effective—opens a Pandora's box of privacy concerns. The fine line between public safety and personal privacy must be tread with caution, ensuring that the pursuit of justice doesn't infringe on individual rights.

The Role of Media

THE ROLE OF MEDIA IN maintaining public interest and pressure in cold cases is undeniable. Yet, there's a need for responsible journalism that respects the privacy and trauma of the victims' families. Sensationalism and intrusive reporting can cause further harm, and it's an ethical imperative for the media to balance their reporting with empathy and respect for those directly affected.

The Psychological Impact

THE PURSUIT OF JUSTICE in cold cases can also have a significant psychological impact on victims' families and survivors. The reopening of old wounds, the roller coaster of hope and despair, and the constant public scrutiny can be emotionally exhausting. There's an ethical responsibility for investigators and the public to respect these emotional burdens and to approach the quest for justice in a manner that minimises potential harm.

In the end, the search for justice in the Zodiac case—or any cold case—is a complex interplay of ethics, law, technology, and human emotion. It's a reminder that while the pursuit of justice is imperative, it must be conducted with respect for the rights of all involved, an awareness of the potential for harm, and a commitment to truth and fairness. The Zodiac case remains a potent symbol of this ongoing quest, encapsulating the hope, determination, and challenges inherent in the journey towards justice and closure.

As we reach the end of our exploration into the chilling mystery of the Zodiac Killer, we find ourselves standing on the precipice of countless questions that still swirl around this case. Each page turned and each chapter closed have unravelled new layers of intrigue, probing into the heart of darkness that encapsulates this enigma. Yet, despite the complexities and challenges we've dissected, one stark truth remains—this story is not yet finished.

We have journeyed together through the haunts of a faceless terror that once lurked in the shadows of America's Golden State, through the chilling letters, the coded messages, and the enduring legacy left in the wake of a killer who evaded capture. We've traversed the landscapes of fear and fascination, of procedural reform and technological innovation, of heartbreaking loss and enduring resilience. We've grappled with the hard questions that the Zodiac case provokes about justice, ethics, and the human capacity for evil.

Yet, despite the elusive resolution, it's the ceaseless pursuit of justice that forms the heart of this story. A quest that has spanned over half a century, passed through countless hands, and left an indelible imprint on criminal investigations. Each breakthrough, every deciphered code, the tireless efforts of law enforcement, amateur sleuths, and resilient survivors are testaments to the indomitable human spirit that refuses to let the Zodiac fade into oblivion.

The narrative of the Zodiac Killer has been as much about the evasive shadow dancing just out of reach as it is about those who chase him—individuals united by their determination to solve the ultimate puzzle, to bring closure to victims' families, and to ensure the memory of those lost is honoured in the annals of history. It is their story that lights the way, even as the Zodiac Killer remains shrouded in darkness.

While we may not have definitive answers or tidy resolutions, one thing is certain—the quest for the truth will continue. As technology advances and new evidence comes to light, the hope for justice remains. The Zodiac case, with its enduring enigma, reminds us that some mysteries persist, but so too does the human drive to solve them.

This is not the end, but a stepping stone on the path of discovery. A point of departure as much as it is a conclusion. As the final page of this book turns, the story of the Zodiac Killer remains open, inviting each of us to keep seeking, to keep questioning, and to never forget the victims and the lessons learned from one of America's most notorious unsolved mysteries.

BEHIND THE MASK: THE ZODIAC KILLER

Thank you for joining me on this journey. Until the day we meet again on the pages of another unsolved mystery, keep the search alive, keep the questions burning, and above all, remember—the search for truth is a quest that never ends.

Don't miss out!

Visit the website below and you can sign up to receive emails whenever Will Anderson publishes a new book. There's no charge and no obligation.

https://books2read.com/r/B-A-TYIZ-VVKLC

BOOKS 2 READ

Connecting independent readers to independent writers.

Also by Will Anderson

Behind The Mask
Behind the Mask: Amanda Knox
Behind the Mask: Jeffrey Dahmer
Behind the Mask: Ted Bundy
Behind the Mask: The Devil's Architect H. H. Holmes
Behind the Mask: The Golden State Killer
Behind the Mask: The Zodiac Killer
Beyond the Headlines: Unraveling the Menendez Brothers

Standalone
The Hatton Garden Heist: Unveiling the Greatest Jewel
Robbery in History

About the Author

Will Anderson is a highly acclaimed author specializing in true crime. His captivating storytelling delves into the dark world of serial killers and unsolved criminal mysteries. The "Behind the Mask" series, his most notable work, peels back the layers of well-known killers, offering an in-depth examination of their twisted minds. Anderson's meticulous research and psychological insights create a gripping reading experience. With an unwavering commitment to truth and justice, he sheds light on cold cases, giving a voice to victims and closure to their families. Will Anderson's contributions to the true crime genre have solidified his place as a respected and sought-after author.

www.ingramcontent.com/pod-product-compliance
Lightning Source LLC
Chambersburg PA
CBHW050601160726
48003CB00002B/995